Let's Meet in Barcelona
A journey through a blend of prose, poetry, and reflection

Gabrijela Šitum

First Edition
Let's Meet in Barcelona
By Gabrijela Šitum
2024, Barcelona, Spain

Illustrations by Víctor Daniel Francia Gómez
Graphic design by Petra Petric
Edited by Hannah Taylor

Website: www.journey-with-gabrijela.com
Email: journeywithgabrijela@gmail.com
ISBN: 978-84-09-65629-5

Disclaimer

This book reflects the author's personal thoughts, experiences, and creative expression. The views expressed are solely those of the author and do not represent any organizations or individuals mentioned.

While some pieces may draw from real events or emotions, they are not meant to depict specific people or situations. Any resemblance to actual persons or events is purely coincidental. The content is intended for literary and artistic purposes and should not be taken as advice or factual accounts.

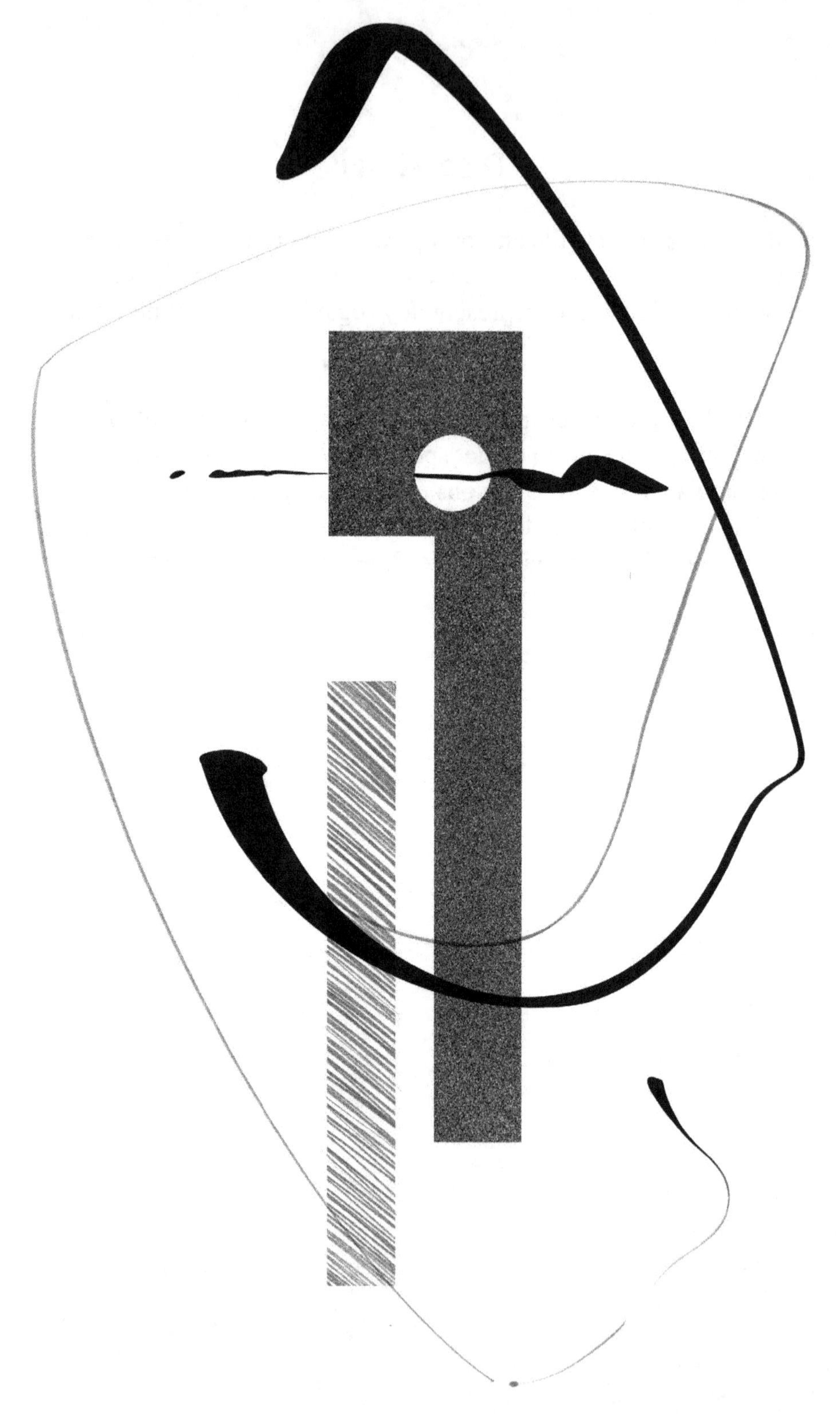

Hello, brave and curious soul

Thank you for deciding to join me on this part of my journey.

This book is about finding love, acceptance, and clarity. It's here to nudge you to be honest with yourself and others, and to motivate you to express what you are going through. I am just like you: Creative, yet hesitant to embrace it because I was taught that creativity was reserved for extraordinary people.

I am not a formally trained writer. I started writing my poems, prose, and essays not so long ago. My native language is Croatian, not English. On top of that, I have dyslexia. Indeed, there were many obstacles in my path to writing this short book.
After so much frustration with learning languages, reading, and writing, I decided to publish this book to prove to myself that I am a writer and maybe inspire someone else to do the same.

For the travelers on the road with me

I have had so much support from my friends, family, teachers, mentors, psychotherapists, and others that I might not have even noticed. I want to thank them all because they helped me get to where I am now.

Table of contents

Welcome

I greeted you with my whole heart.
I listened to you with excitement,
eager to meet and understand you.

I looked at you with admiration.
I believed your words, not your actions.
I called you, hoping you would listen to
my needs.

I wondered if you ever thought about me.
I cared because I saw potential.
I hugged you, thinking
you would heal more quickly.

I gave in because I trusted you.
I loved you because I had enough love to give.
I expected a lot
and was disappointed many times.

I hoped that what we had in my head was real.
I even saw us having children together.
I stayed because you needed me,
and I needed you.

I waited for you because you needed space.
But this was just one stop on both of our journeys.

One thing I didn't do was dream because my
instinct didn't allow me.
People come and go. That is how we grow.
Learn from everyone, and welcome a few.

You know where the door is,
I would appreciate it if you left

After they set flames to my walls,
After an earthquake shook my foundation,
When I was at my lowest,
When cracks appeared in every corner of my shelter,
When I had so many doubts about my

Strength,

Structure,

Worth.

When friends were few,
When my comfort zone became solitude,

Why didn't you dare to ask how I was?
What are you doing here again, entering my life?

Now,
When I feel better,
When I am at a high point,
When I know exactly what I want and need.

Are you here to ask me what my plans are and how
you could support me?
Are you here to ask me if I've created
something new lately that I am proud of?
Are you here to say how proud you are of me?
Are you here to be my shelter where I can rest?

Or

Are you here to waste my time?
Are you here to distract me?
Are you here to ignore me again after giving me breadcrumbs?
Are you here because you don't have anyone else?

Why are you so selfish?

You know where the door is, I would appreciate it if you left

Why are you causing me so much

Pain,

Grief,

Sadness?

This is not me.
I want my

Shiny,

Bubbly,

Childish side to break free again.

Please don't waste my time if your intention is not to help me

Thrive,

Glow, and

Bloom.

If you don't want to be here next to me,
seeing me grow,
watching me reach my full potential,
making my day, creating a safe space —

If you don't want to share my home both when it's messy and
when it's newly furnished —

The door is there.
Leave my house.

Dance with others, but
don't forget to dance alone

Last year, I discovered myself by meeting other people.
I was an excellent companion to all of them.

Some of them gave me a good vibe,
    with others, something was off.
Some of them fulfilled me,
    others drained me.
Some of them served me,
    others didn't at all.
Some of them inspired me,
    and others pulled me into depression.
Some of them loved me,
    and others used me.
Some of them wanted the best for me,
    and others didn't.
Some of them were honest,
    and others weren't.
Some of them broke my heart.

I broke some hearts along the way —

Some of them brought out my best side,
> others my worst.
Some of them nourished my feminine side,
> others my masculine side.
Some of them brought a smile to my face,
> others tears.
Some of them gave me clear directions,
> and others confused me.
Some of them sparked excitement in me,
> others boredom.
Some of them gave me a feeling of security,
> others insecurity.
Some of them gave me hope,
> others despair.
Some of them made me feel seen,
> others misunderstood.
Some of them made me feel accepted,
> others rejected.
Some of them made me feel appreciated,
> others unappreciated.
Some of them found time for me when I was in need,
> others didn't.
Some of them accepted me,
> and others thought I was crazy.

Some of them brought me happiness,
       others made me feel lonely.
Some of them I connected with deeply.

I didn't connect with others.

My heart and soul are tired and broken
and need to recharge.
I gave a part of me to all of them because they needed to be
understood.
I accepted them as they were. While doing that, I was accepting
parts of me, not them.

Now, it is time to let some of them go,
to let some parts of myself go.
It is hard to let go of some of the beliefs and principles that have
been here all my life, but I know I will feel relief.

I need to protect my heart and my energy to create greater things
and become my best self.

Before dancing with others, I want to dance with myself.

Who or what would you like to invite into your life, and how would you like to feel in their presence?

Echoes of Communication

When you speak and feel unheard,
When you listen, but the meaning wavers,
When you act in kindness, and it goes
unnoticed,
You speak clearly, yet the echo returns empty.

Among all the languages — love, giving, crafts,
cultures, gestures — Could it be that we share
nothing in common?

Have you listened to your own voice above the
noise?
Have you understood the silence beneath
your poise?

With some, I share a tongue but not a thought,
With others, no words are exchanged, yet
understanding is caught. It is magical the
moment a stranger's eyes meet mine,
words may be lost,
yet I feel seen.

I shine.

It seems that what is unseen is what connects
us.
There must be invisible waves that touch the
mind and heart.

Next time you meet someone, ask yourself:
Do you hear your own echo, or does the
person truly absorb not just your words but
also the silent languages you speak?

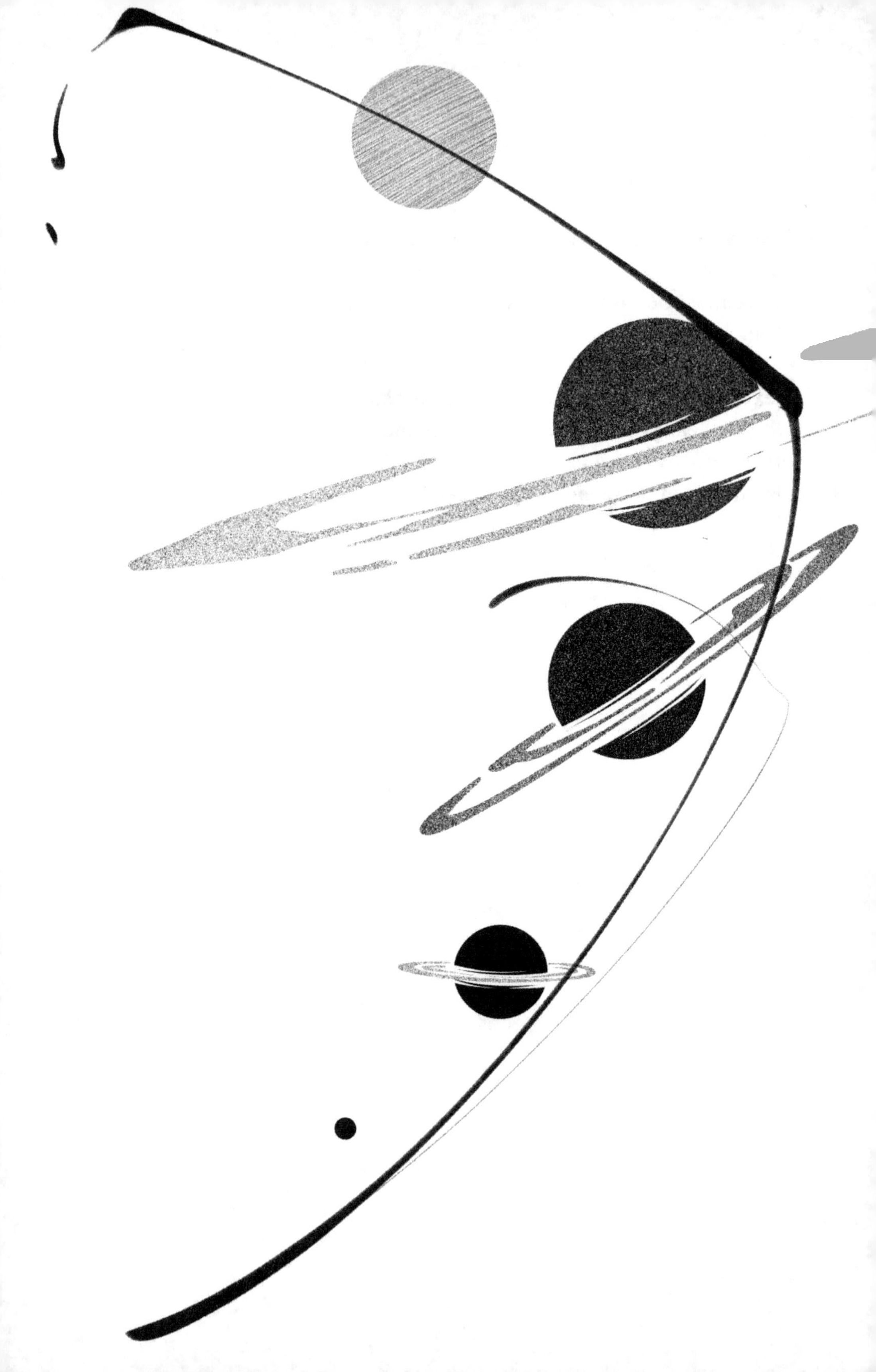

"What time is it?" I asked.
"Time to explode," said the sun.

There's the sun!
Can you see it?
Can you feel it?
Can you sense it?

In the background, you can hear breathing, deep breaths. You can sense life, smell freshness, the smell of Spring.

My sun.

I can see it from a distance.

It is beautiful.
It is peaceful, giving me a sense of purpose and joy.
It is powerful.
It is full of positive energy, motivation, and inspiration.
It is so wise.
It guides me, talks to me, and nurtures me.

"What time is it?" was the question that popped into my mind just before it exploded. It seemed like it was time for new life, new beginnings, new chances.

*There is the sound of an explosion, but as if it were
in the sea, a muffled and distant sound.*

I didn't panic. I didn't cry. I wasn't sad.
I felt at peace. I felt excited, as if something new
was coming.
It might take a couple of moments, months, or
years for the sun to start shining again, but I have a
feeling it will be even more magnificent.
It had to fall into pieces.
It had to expand and transform.
Only then could I understand what it was made of.

Sun, I will pick up all the pieces. I know you are
going to reassemble.
The world and you might be different when we get
all the pieces together. Don't worry, everything is
going to fall into order. You will shine again, even
brighter.

What untapped potential within you is ready to come alive?

In a new skin after so many burning wounds

I smelled my skin burning.
The parts of my body I admire the most were
wounded. They were visible and uncomfortable, but
I wasn't ashamed because I knew that new, young,
healed skin would show after the old one peeled
off.
The biggest, most painful burns were on my heart
and in my stomach because of the acidity of your
apathy.

Did you know that even when I smile, explore
new things, and am busy, I sometimes feel sad and
lonely?

I wanted to be with you so much that I dishonored
myself by thinking that maybe I don't need
someone who is going to take care of me
consistently.
I lowered my standards to the point that I forgot
what I wanted and what I was searching for.
Thanks for showing me how my lowest looks.

We are done here.
I am not getting lower than this. From this
point, I can only go higher.

Watch me and my new, young, shiny, healed
skin touch new places,
opportunities,
hearts,
and milestones.

I lost my love for my old home so that I could build a new one

It feels like I've lost my love for my old home.
It doesn't feel like home anymore, even
though I thought it would be my forever.
The elevator is broken, and I often find myself
struggling for air. Some neighbors have been
hurt trying to reach their apartments, as if
the walls themselves are closing in. The light
that once flooded through the windows now
barely reaches inside. It feels as if the sun has
shifted, leaving the rooms in constant shadow.
Everything feels heavier now.
Nothing is permanent, it seems, but
everything is here for a specific period of
time. Now, as I'm leaving, I feel a bit nostalgic.
I remember moments of joy.
I feel that I have drifted off the track and need
to find a new path. I close my eyes and begin
to imagine what my new home will look like.

I am homesick for the home I am creating — a house of
dance, play, and creativity, balanced with calmness and
laughter and infused with the scent of pine trees by the
summer seaside.
A full house filled with light, love, and excitement. A place
full of living art, my art, surrounded by loved ones. A table
laden with delightful dishes and soul-stirring drinks. Our
conversations flow effortlessly, like a dance without rules.
Looking at myself in the mirror, I can't help but smile,
feeling happy and proud of the life I'm leading. I know my
younger self would be proud, too.
The blending of blue and red into purple, like the morning
mist, energizes me to start each day fresh, positive, and full
of vitality.
Stepping outside, I take in the view, and the chorus of birds,
the lush greenery, and the sea. I breathe deeply, savoring
the fresh morning air. Here, the sun always shines, and
children's laughter, pure and joyful, brings smiles to all.

Life is not too short, it is long enough to do what I want.
I lost my love for my old home so that I could build
a new one.

Time

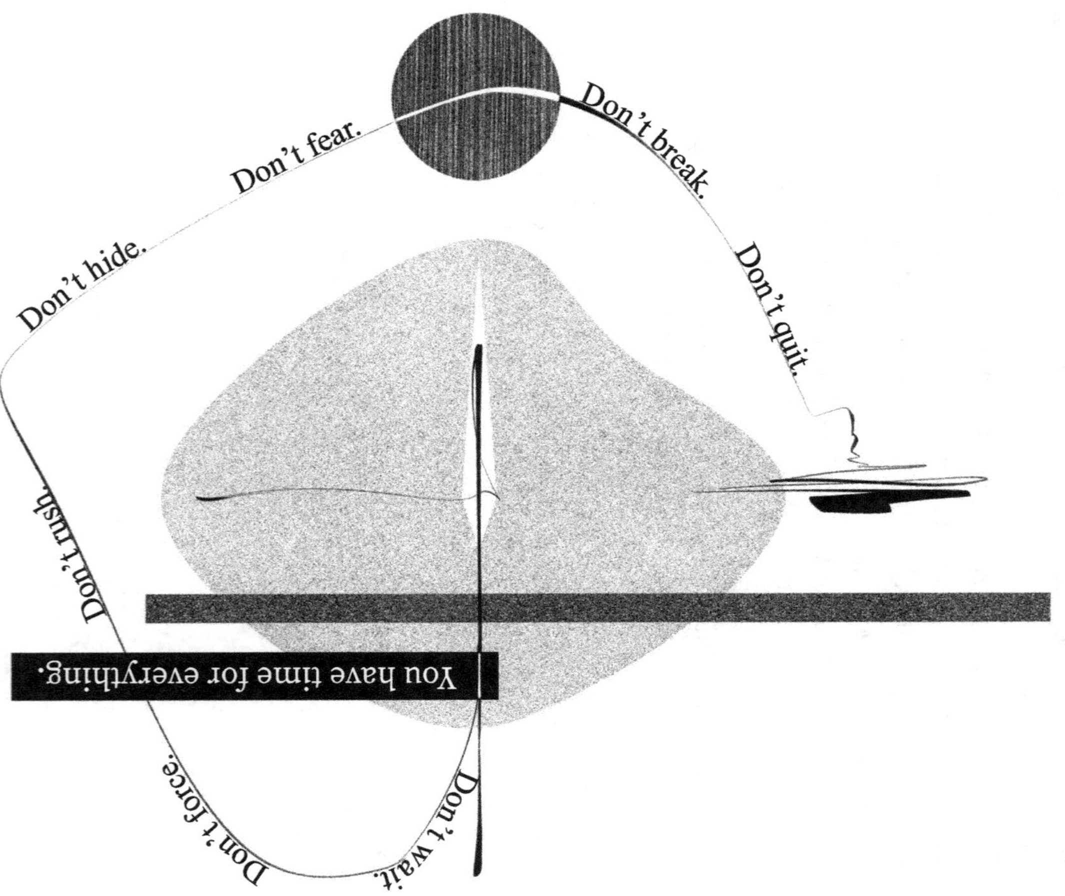

Don't fear.
Don't break.
Don't hide.
Don't quit.
Don't rush.
Don't force.
Don't wait.
You have time for everything.

Just do it

Come rain or shine.
One path or another.
Speak up or stay silent.
Act now or delay.
Is this truth or fiction?

There is no right or wrong.
There is no good or bad.
There is just perception.
There is just what you do and decide.
What, then, will you choose?

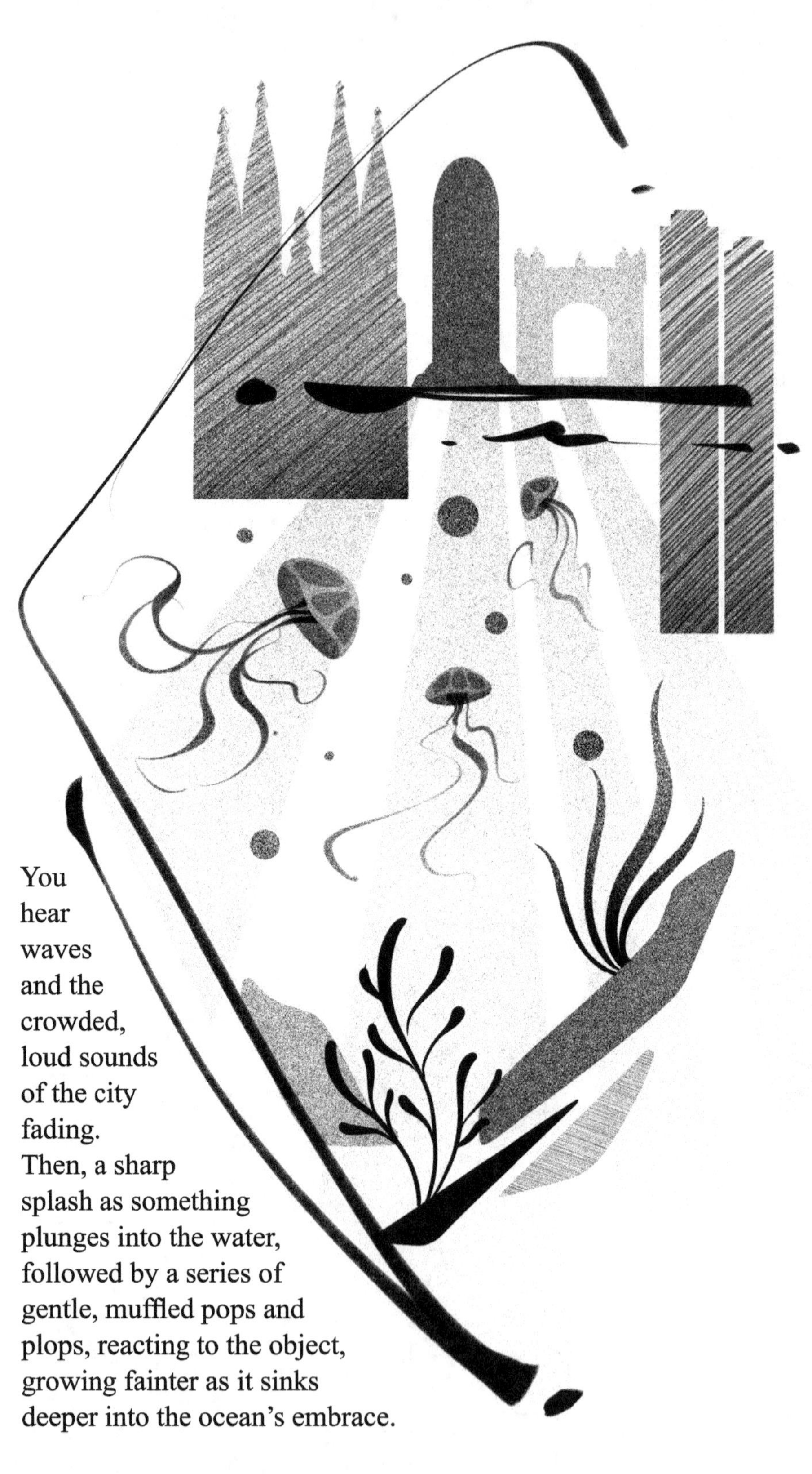

You
hear
waves
and the
crowded,
loud sounds
of the city
fading.
Then, a sharp
splash as something
plunges into the water,
followed by a series of
gentle, muffled pops and
plops, reacting to the object,
growing fainter as it sinks
deeper into the ocean's embrace.

Let it go, breathe, and
go with the flow

Where am I?
Do I know how to breathe here?
Am I drowning?

Exhausted from fighting for my life and panicking about how
to breathe and where to go, I decided to let go, surrender to the
ocean, and trust it.

"I have only one wish," I said,
"please keep my lungs and heart safe."

And soon, my breath adjusted,
and I felt my heartbeat,
but I still couldn't talk.

Even before my sight and hearing adjusted,
I could feel life, excitement, and opportunities.

With every moment, I felt more and more as if I belonged here.
Each day, I felt more like myself.

It is time for me to heal, to recover.
It is time for me to rest, to drift, and not to
burn myself out.
It is time for me to surrender and trust the
waves and currents.

Now is the time for me to observe and
recognize opportunities and see which one
resonates with me.
If it doesn't feel right, I don't have to reach for
it. I can just let the sea's flow guide me to the
next one.

Hey, beautiful creature, please don't force
your ideas onto my mind, don't undermine
my beliefs, and don't manipulate my thoughts.

Don't you dare change my focus!

I have my defences. My intention is not
to hurt you as long as you respect my
boundaries, dreams, and emotions.

Show respect, and don't interrupt me while
I explore the depths, as I glide smoothly
through this new world.
You are welcome to join me.
I would love that, but keep in mind that I can
sense your intentions, so you better be honest
about why you want to take this journey with
me.

＊

Dear ocean,
I am so happy you are so vast.
I am so grateful for your invitation.
I am fascinated by your endless mystery.

＊

I know exactly what I want, how I want to
feel, and the impact I want to create.
I don't know how I will get there, because the
ocean is unpredictable and full of surprises.
But still, I feel safe in it.
And I trust the ocean will get me there.

My Definition of Strength

I am so strong.
I can do everything alone,
but I don't want to anymore.

I am strong,
not because I am independent,
even though many see me that way.
I need a break,
for someone to drive.

I just need a moment —
a moment to change the definition of what
being strong means.

I am strong only
because I care,
because I am gentle,
and because I am honest.

I am strong
because I am able to ask for what I need
and stand up for myself.

I am strong
because I ask for help.

I don't want to be the type of hero
who sacrifices myself for others.

Yes, I will help.
I will listen.
I will be there for others.
But above all,
I want to be a hero
who stands up for myself first.

On the run

I had been sprinting for hours. It felt like
years. The clock chimed to mark a new hour
so many times that I lost count. It was my
mundane activity.

Damn it, I grazed my knee on one of the trees,
reminding me that I was in a dense forest.
I didn't stop. I just looked at the trees and
saw that they were all peeling. Then, a hard
sound. Bang. I knocked my head on one of the
trees, chipping my front tooth.

I never saw that coming. I fell on my back and
looked up, seeing a crooked branch. I hoped
it wouldn't fall and crush me before I stood up
and continued running.

I hate running, but I don't know why.
I believe we have all the answers.
I believe that if we are honest with ourselves
and listen to ourselves, we will achieve much
more and faster.
But we are so afraid of the truth.

The truth that is inside us, the truth we see
when talking to others, the truth we see when
trying to understand the world's standards
and expectations. What I saw last year was a
lot of people running, not only me.

Some people run in the park, do marathons
and triathlons, and others catch a bus or jump
into a new career. Some people run to another
place on Earth to find something, not even
knowing what they are searching for.
I ran for many reasons, but now I see myself
running to different activities to explore and
to keep me busy, procrastinating instead of
doing what I know I should be doing.

I hope all of us runners breathe enough air
and stay hydrated. I am thirsty like the plants
in Barcelona's parks during the summer
drought. The drink I'd been drinking didn't
hydrate me. In fact, it had made me even
thirstier. But still, I continued running.

That's enough of running to find, catch, or run
away from… What are you running away from?

I will stop for a moment to rest. Who knows?
Maybe someone will pass by, sit next to me,
and offer me the drink that will help me stay
hydrated.

Appreciating Acts

The fun side of life is learning.
We can learn from parrots —
they adapt to new environments,
Mimic the world around them,
but still stay true to their nature.
They squawk and dance,
showing off their colors without fear,
Loving loudly, sharing openly, and creating
space for others.

The collective is as important as support.
We are individuals, but never alone.

Are we boring as individuals,
or are we bored without a community,
or neither?
You tell me.

We can be like parrots,
finding joy in the crowd,
Yet still shining on our own.
I'm the kind of person who thinks I'm special.

But the truth is that there are billions of people
like me.
I hope you are one of them.
I hope you love yourself, and that you create
something worth sharing.

You can't fool me.
True acts of kindness, of character —
they're rare.
But just like a parrot's bright feathers in a flock,
There are individuals who stand out.

Soothe yourself.
There are millions of us,
bright souls waiting to be seen.
Like I said — nobody is that special,
But maybe we should be louder,
like the parrots.

Where are you all?
If nobody appreciates your acts, I will.
And people like me, there are many of us.
Show yourself.

Reflections

The next time you make a decision or take
action,
ask yourself how it will make someone else
feel,
someone you care about.

Our selfishness has reached its peak.
Poor communication kills relationships,
creating disappointments.
Immediate satisfaction and dopamine
cravings
prevent long-lasting connections.

Having so many choices
paralyzes our ability to choose.
This message isn't just for you. It's for me too.

Our flexibility blurs who we are.
Our priorities are forgotten.
Yet, hope keeps us motivated.
Should life be easier?

What if love isn't the problem?
What if my identity isn't lost?

What if my job is just a job?
What if I don't need to achieve grand things?

What if I'm here to observe, react, and create?
What if I'm here to make others feel
important, not myself?
What if I'm here to give others what they need
in ways they don't expect?

Questions keep me moving,
improving, growing,
but still, I don't know the answers.

Where in your life do you need to create space for rest and renewal?

Unconditional Naivety

I was too naive, thinking that unconditional
love exists.
We all expect something.
Unconditional love will be reached only if we
all share love and have pure intentions and
actions toward each other.
I don't see that in reality. Do you?

Never mind,
what I wanted to say was that I am naive.
I trust people too easily.
I let go of myself the first moment I sense that
a person has something good in them,
and there is good in all the people I meet.
At least, I like to believe that.

All of this has led me to the point where I
have trust issues.
I would love to believe people.
I would love to go with the flow
and let myself go,
But lately, my gut has been sending me more
and more alerts.

So, unfortunately, from now on my trust
needs to be earned.

Why?

Why can't we all just have pure hearts and
intentions?
What brought us here?
Am I the only one who wants to believe
people are generally good and trust them?

Though I often face disappointment, each
lesson learned fuels my inspiration to create
meaningful art.
But is the inspiration worth the struggle?

Sand Everywhere

Sand is everywhere.
Even if you want to,
you can't get rid of it.

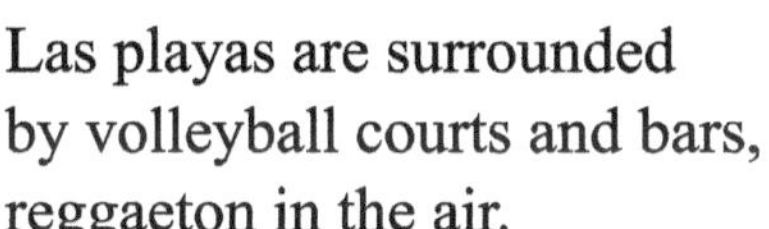

Las playas are surrounded
by volleyball courts and bars,
reggaeton in the air.

A girl in a bikini sways,
her curves eclipsing the horizon.

"Agua, cerveza, water, beer,"
echoes from all directions.

Calming waves hit the sand,
sounding like they're stuck in a loop.
Foreigners talk about good vibes in the city,
unaware they're projecting the vibe.

Sand clings to salty skin.
I can't tell if my skin is salty from the sea
or sweat.
Some faces seem familiar — Maybe from
yesterday,
past lives,
dreams,
or Bumble.
Who knows.

Sombrillas close,
the sun sets,
people leave,
but sand remains everywhere.

Let's Meet in Barcelona

Comb my hair,
the most precious, soft thing you've touched.
Don't be ashamed.

Don't stop looking at me with your deep, dark
brown eyes,
Full of curiosity, love, and admiration.

Love me with your acts, words, time, body,
and soul.

Don't let me go,
even when I'm scared of love,
When I feel insecure
or when I might push you away.

I'm sorry for being so weird about it.

Please hold me, keep me safe, and be honest.
You don't need to change.
I don't want that.
You need to be honest.

I want to download your past,
knowledge, and experience,
To get all the insights I missed,
To get to know you better.

Let's meet where you are.
Let's meet where I am.
I hope it's the same place.
Let's meet in Barcelona.

What do your recent actions reveal about your priorities, and how might they be impacting those you care about?

What environments or experiences do you find yourself drawn back to, even when they linger like sand — familiar and comforting, yet inescapable?

Final Thoughts

When you see me tired, walking, or taking time for a siesta,
it's because I decided to turn the autopilot off and embrace the
discomfort of manual control. Yes, I sweat more, and I need much
more rest. But I've also learned so much about the world and
myself, and I can see how fast I've grown.

I hope this book has sparked something in you and that you have
enjoyed parts of my journey. Now, maybe it's time for you to write
your own. I would love to hear from you. Feel free to share your
thoughts with me. My email is journeywithgabrijela@gmail.com,
and my website is www.journey-with-gabrijela.com.
If nobody else is your cheerleader, I can be.

Enjoy the journey,
Gabrijela